The Story Of The
Tamarack

Tobias Clarke

Illustrated by Jeffrey Wilson

Tellwell Talent
www.tellwell.ca

ISBN
978-0-2288-0935-7 (Hardcover)
978-0-2288-0934-0 (Paperback)

Tobias Clarke: I would like to dedicate this story to Morgan, Madeline and Colin. The three most important people in my life.

Jeffrey Wilson: I would like to dedicate the illustrations to my parents, wife, children and grand-children.

It was a bright, crisp fall morning in the small town of White Otter Lake. Rosette and her *moushoum* were walking down the old dirt road toward their favourite fishing spot. Rosette was 10 years old, but she was very small for her age; she had to hurry to keep up with her grandfather, who was tall and strong.

Rosette liked these early morning adventures with Moushoum. She was very curious about all living things on Mother Earth and Moushoum never seemed to tire of her many questions. Moushoum loved these moments, too. He enjoyed sharing his teachings with his inquisitive little grandchild. But this day turned out to be even more special, because Rosette saw something she had never seen before.

When they were almost at their fishing spot, Rosette stopped and pointed up at the many rows of trees with brown needles. "Moushoum, what is wrong with those trees?" she asked, looking up as tears filled her eyes. "Why are they sick?"

Rosette's tears began spilling over her lashes and down her plump rosy cheeks. Moushoum bent down to her, holding out his arms. Wrapping them securely around his beloved granddaughter, he cradled her lovingly and said, "Now Rosette, don't cry for those trees. They are not sick. They are here to remind us that we are all here on Mother Earth to take care of one another."

Confused and still sobbing, Rosette looked up at her grandfather and asked, "How, Moushoum? I don't understand."

"Come, sit with me here," Moushoum said, as he guided her to an old, well-worn log and sat her down gently. "I will tell you the story of the Tamarack."

"Many years ago, the tamarack tree was the greatest of all the needle trees across the lands. It could see as far as the eye could see. The Tamarack was the one tree that all needle trees wished to be reborn as one day. But sometimes, when living things in this world believe they are the greatest, they can become selfish. They forget they still must be kind and caring to all living things on Mother Earth. They must remember that in the Creator's eyes, they are no bigger than the smallest of all living things. The Tamarack forgot this lesson."

Rosette sat on the log with her feet crossed, listening with wide eyes and open ears. Her moushoum smiled and continued.

"It was the end of a cold fall season and Winter had surprised Fall with a great storm. Many animals needed to seek shelter from Winter's fury and rage. A lot of them found a safe place to wait while the storm ripped through the lands, but some could not find safety in time.

"A flock of birds had flown into the storm, which had come without warning, and they were caught in the strong winds. They flapped their wings ferociously, but to no avail. They could no longer continue their travels. Their wings were tired, and they needed a place to rest while the storm passed. Then, the birds saw the tall Tamarack trees and began to fly to the safety of the mighty trees' limbs. They were only a few feet away from reaching safety when something terrible happened.

"The Tamaracks' limbs began to move, wrapping tightly around their massive trunks. They were trying to stop the flock from landing on them. With their great limbs tightly wound around their trunks, the Tamaracks then shouted, 'Go away birds, we are tired and getting ready for our winter sleep. We will not be disturbed with your squawking on our branches. You are not welcome here. Now go away!'

"The birds pleaded with the Tamaracks, begging for help, but the Tamaracks still refused. Rather than finding safety among the branches, the flock was forced to continue flying in the harsh weather, looking for another place to wait out the blistering storm.

"Now, the Tamaracks were happy they had sent the birds away. They felt they were too important to be disturbed. They were, after all, the greatest trees in all the forests.

"What the Tamaracks did not know was that the Great Spirit had been watching. The Great Spirit was sad and disappointed with the Tamaracks, for the Tamaracks had been given their greatness so they could protect the smallest of living creatures. They were given their mighty limbs so many two-winged friends could rest on them between their long flights. The Tamaracks had also been gifted with soft, featherlike needles to provide warmth for their guests who sat on their branches. But the Tamaracks had become selfish and uncaring. They felt they were above all things on Mother Earth.

"The Great Spirit came down to face the Tamaracks and proclaimed, 'Tamaracks! I gifted you your greatness, but today you showed me your spirit is far from great. You turned away your two-winged friends when they needed you most, and for this you will be forever changed. For all eternity, you will feel the cold and pain your friends felt today. No longer will you have needles to protect you on the coldest days. You will lose your warm, feathery winter coat, for every autumn your needles will die and fall to Mother Earth's floor. Naked, you will suffer the harsh, biting winds that Winter blows on you. And, you will no longer be able to close your branches, as they will shoot out straight and never bend. You will never again believe you are greater than the smallest living creature, as you are all equal in my eyes.' With that, the Great Spirit left the Tamaracks on that cold, stormy day, hoping the trees would learn their lesson.

"Hundreds of moons passed over the trees, and the Tamaracks began to accept the changes that had been given to them. They started to grow smaller in the forests, so they could seek shelter among the other trees when the Spirit of Winter came to visit. Their wood also became extremely strong since the Great Spirit changed the way their branches grew.

"Then a day came upon the Tamaracks they could have never imagined. A young man was walking in the heat of summer and became tired. He decided to rest beneath the Tamaracks, and within moments he was fast asleep. While the man slept he was gifted with a vision of walking up hills that were difficult to climb. He saw himself with a walking stick that helped him like a trusted friend. Then the man heard the softest voice say, 'I am Tamarack. With my strong limbs, I can help you. I would be honoured to be your friend. I am who you rest upon now.'

"Startled, the man awoke from his sleep and looked up at the Tamarack he had been resting under. He raised himself up and examined the tree more closely. He could tell this was a tree of great strength. With the Tamarack's permission, the man pulled an axe from his pack and began to chop the Tamarack down. The man spent hours chopping away, until what he had before him was a strong, beautifully carved walking stick. It was at that moment, the friendship he had dreamt of began.

"The young man and his Tamarack travelled the world. They went to places as far as the eye could see. The Tamarack was at peace again and was filled with gratitude towards their new friend.

"Then a day came when the Great Spirit spoke through the bustling wind to his needled friend, the Tamarack.

"'My great friend, you have seen the errors of your past ways, so this is my gift to you. You will stay the same way you are today, but you will once again see as far as the eye can see. You have great friends who need your strength, and you will join them on their many journeys. You will never be above or below anyone again, as you will now walk beside them. You will never be alone.'

"The Tamarack thanked the Great Spirit for all that had been done for them. So the Tamarack continued to walk Mother Earth beside their new friend."

Rosette jumped from her spot on the log and ran from Moushoum towards the Tamaracks. She stretched her arms out as wide as she could and hugged them around one of the trees.

"Thank you, Tamarack! *Miigwetch!* You may be smaller now, but you are greater than you have ever been."

Rosette continued to hug the Tamarack, when suddenly a voice came out of the air and spoke to her and Moushoum.

"My friend Rosette, can you take me with you, so you can share my story? For I would be honoured to walk beside you."

Rosette and Moushoum looked at each other in surprise and smiled. Rosette patted the side of the great tree and said in her most stoic voice, "Yes, my new friend, but it is I who am honoured to walk beside you."

THE END

24

About The Author

Tobias Clarke is an oral storyteller and has always enjoyed the lessons learned from traditional stories. She is a Drummond Island Metis descendant and is an active Metis community member in Ontario.

Over the years she has developed a deep connection with her Metis culture, and has been recognized for her traditional knowledge and teachings.

THE STORY OF THE TAMARACK is her first step towards taking her oral storytelling to the next level. The young Metis girl in the story is named after one of Tobias' Metis ancestors. She wrote her interpretation of this story back in 2011 and kept it in her dresser drawer until now.

About The Illustrator

Jeffrey Wilson, a descendent of Metis heritage, began to draw at an early age on a Grey County, Ontario farm, dreaming of one day having his work in the newspaper funnies. After many years and scribbles later, the dream came to fruition when his comics, gags and editorial panels began to appear in publications across Canada.

Jeff branched out to become a key animator in the 1986-87 "The Adventures of Teddy Ruxpin" animated TV series, and amid a myriad of vocations, has spent almost two decades years as a newspaper graphic artist at Grey County's last community broadsheet, The Dundalk Herald.

Jeffrey came to Tobias' attention when he illustrated daughter Rebekah Wilson's book, "The Tiny Voyageur" (Friesen Press). Today, he and wife Barb are rarely at their central Grey County home, absorbed in work, grandkids, or hobbies of improv comedy and community theatre.

CPSIA information can be obtained
at www.ICGtesting.com
Printed in the USA
BVHW022325150422
634376BV00002B/12